FOSSIL FILES

AMPHIBIAN FOSSILS

MARIEL BARD

PowerKiDS
press.

NEW YORK

Published in 2017 by The Rosen Publishing Group, Inc.
29 East 21st Street, New York, NY 10010

First Edition

Editor: Melissa Raé Shofner
Book Design: Tanya Dellaccio

Photo Credits: Cover (frog fossil) John Cancalosi/Getty Images; cover, back cover, p. 1 (file folder) Victoria Kalinina/Shutterstock.com; p. 5 Ken Lucas/Getty Images; p. 7 LuFeeTheBear/Shutterstock.com; p. 7 (limnocelis fossil) Ken Schafer/Getty Images; p. 9 (elginerpeton) https://commons.wikimedia.org/wiki/File:Elginerpeton_BW.jpg; p. 9 (Per Ahlberg) Jonathan Blair/Getty Images; p. 11 Galyna Andrushko/Shutterstock.com; p. 13 Courtesy of Oregon State University Flickr; p. 15 Jason Patrick Ross/Shutterstock.com; p. 15 (sandstone footprints) https://commons.wikimedia.org/wiki/File:Coconino_Sandstone_with_footprints.jpg; p. 16 https://commons.wikimedia.org/wiki/File:Mucrospirifer_mucronatus_Silica_Shale.JPG; pp. 17, 25 (fossil) De Agostini Picture Library/DeAgostini/Getty Images; p. 19 MarcelClemens/Shutterstock.com; p. 21 (fossil) Gerobatrachus hottoni Anderson et al., 2008/PAL489135; p. 21 (gerobatrachus) https://commons.wikimedia.org/wiki/File:Gerobatrachus_NT.jpg; p. 23 Helen H. Richardson/Denver Post/Getty Images; p. 23 (tiger salamander) Matt Jeppson/Shutterstock.com; p. 25 (3d rendering) 3drenderings/Shutterstock.com; p. 27 Richard A McMillin/Shutterstock.com; p. 27 (fossil) https://commons.wikimedia.org/wiki/File:Eryops_-_National_Museum_of_Natural_History_-_IMG_1974.JPG; p. 29 (eocaecilia) https://commons.wikimedia.org/wiki/File:Eocaecilia_BW.jpg; p. 29 (caecilian) R. Andrew Odum/Getty Images.

Cataloging-in-Publication Data
Names: Bard, Mariel.
Title: Amphibian fossils / Mariel Bard.
Description: New York : PowerKids Press, 2017. | Series: Fossil files | Includes index.
Identifiers: ISBN 9781499427202 (pbk.) | ISBN 9781499428629 (library bound) | ISBN 9781499427219 (6 pack)
Subjects: LCSH: Fossils–Juvenile literature.
Classification: LCC QE714.5 B37 2017 | DDC 560–dc23

Manufactured in the United States of America

CPSIA Compliance Information: Batch Batch #BW17PK: For Further Information contact Rosen Publishing, New York, New York at 1-800-237-9932

CONTENTS

WHAT ARE FOSSILS?

Did you know that some kinds of animals you see today—such as frogs, toads, newts, and salamanders—have actually been around for millions of years? They may have looked a little different back then, but their modern-day relatives are currently hopping and crawling around!

Many amphibians that lived long ago were preserved as fossils. Fossils are the traces or hardened remains of dead plants or animals. They can stay buried for millions of years until someone comes along and digs them up. Paleontologists are scientists who actively search for fossils.

Fossils are snapshots of the past. They offer clues about how ancient organisms lived hundreds of millions of years ago. They also help scientists understand how species alive today have **evolved**.

Dig It!

The English word "fossil" comes from the Latin word *fossilis*, which means "dug up."

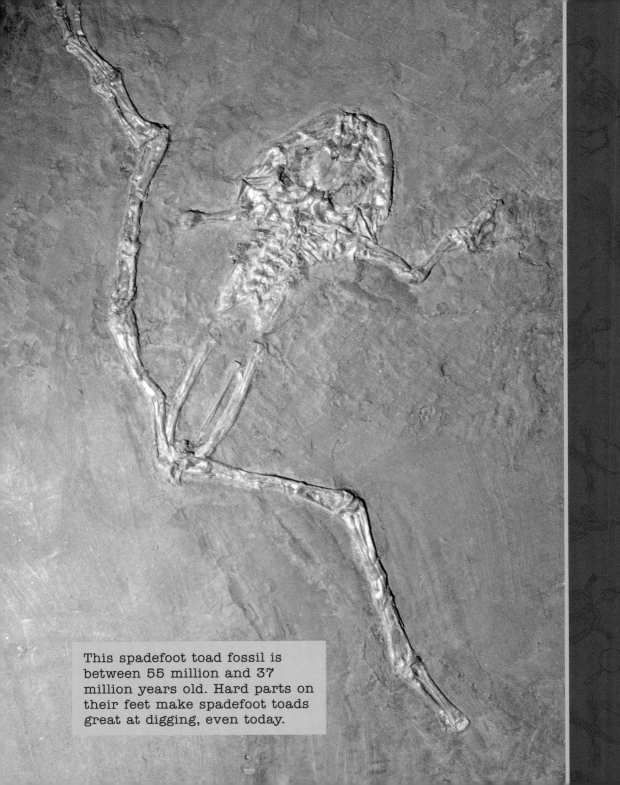

This spadefoot toad fossil is between 55 million and 37 million years old. Hard parts on their feet make spadefoot toads great at digging, even today.

PALEONTOLOGY

Paleontology is the study of plants and animals that lived many years ago. Paleontologists study fossils. They need to know a lot about geology (the study of rocks) and biology (the study of life and living organisms) in order to re-create and understand the past. They look for fossils all around the world to better understand where and when ancient life existed, what it was like, and how it changed over time.

Amphibians are an exciting group of organisms for paleontologists to study. They start their lives in water but later split their time between water and dry land. This gives paleontologists multiple types of locations to search for fossils. Studying amphibians also allows scientists to better understand the evolution from water-based life on Earth to land-based life on Earth.

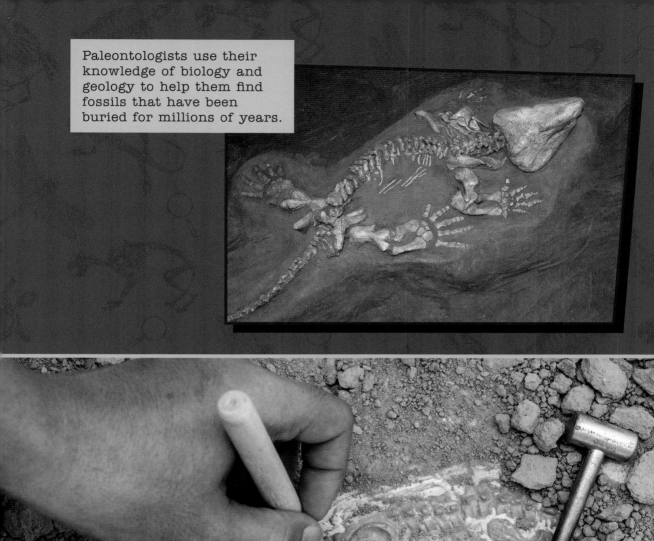

Paleontologists use their knowledge of biology and geology to help them find fossils that have been buried for millions of years.

THE FIRST AMPHIBIAN FOSSIL

The earliest discovered amphibian fossil is *Elginerpeton pancheni*. It was found in Scotland in the 1800s and is about 368 million years old. At first, scientists didn't really know what sort of creature it was. Only a few parts of the animal's skeleton had been found.

In the early 1990s, a paleontologist named Dr. Per Ahlberg reexamined the fossil. He determined that it was a tetrapod, which is a four-limbed **vertebrate**. Usually scientists recognize tetrapods by their limbs, but there are other ways to identify them. Dr. Ahlberg noted certain things about *Elginerpeton pancheni's* jaw that are commonly found in modern tetrapods. Today's amphibians are also tetrapods. This discovery helped fill in a major gap in our understanding of their evolution. However, scientists still aren't sure exactly where *Elginerpeton pancheni* belongs in the amphibian family tree.

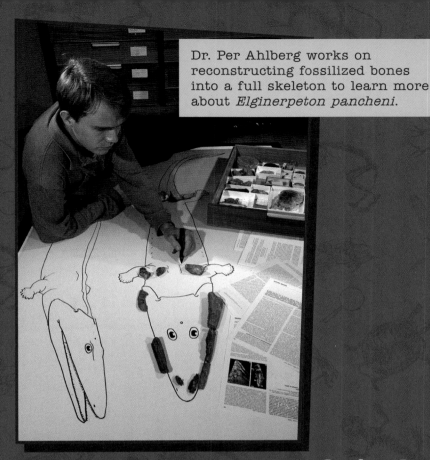

Dr. Per Ahlberg works on reconstructing fossilized bones into a full skeleton to learn more about *Elginerpeton pancheni.*

They're Not Related

Though some parts of their bodies may look or function very similarly, amphibians are not related to reptiles. Both of these types of animal evolved from fish, but they evolved separately. One major difference between reptiles and amphibians is that amphibians usually have soft, wet skin. Reptiles have hard parts called scales on their bodies. For many amphibians, their soft skin is their main way of breathing rather than using lungs or gills.

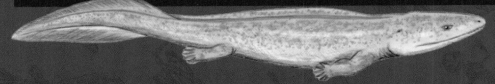

rendering of *Elginerpeton pancheni*

FOSSIL FORMATION

Some fossils form when an organism dies and its remains are changed into stone. Shortly after an organism dies, its remains are covered in **sediment**. This protects it from things like harsh weather or scavengers. Over time, the organism's soft body parts break down and its bones are replaced by solid rock. Most amphibian fossils form this way.

Organisms are sometimes preserved in amber, which is a hardened type of tree resin. This happens when a small creature gets trapped in the sticky resin. When the resin solidifies, it preserves the animal fully intact, soft tissues and all. A very small tree frog was found preserved in amber in 2007. Scientists think the frog lived around 25 million years ago.

Dig It!

Ancient amphibians sometimes left trackway fossils. These are fossils that show a creature's footprints and sometimes the tracks left by its dragging tail or belly.

A tiny frog is shown perfectly preserved in amber. People sometimes wear amber as jewelry, including pieces with fossilized organisms inside!

Rare Finds

Only a small number of ancient organisms have been preserved as fossils. Hard skeletons or shells make it much more likely for a fossil to form. Soft-bodied organisms, such as jellyfish, will almost never leave a fossil. Small animals trapped in amber (such as an insect or a frog) or in ice (such as a mammoth) are two rare examples of organisms being completely preserved.

TRAPPED IN AMBER!

It's pretty rare to find an entire organism preserved in amber. It's also rare to find a fossilized salamander. So it was quite a find when a biologist discovered a 20-million-year-old salamander trapped in amber!

The little creature lived in what is now the Dominican Republic, a nation in the Caribbean Sea. This is important because, while common to North America, salamanders aren't found on the Caribbean islands today. This means salamanders once lived much farther south than scientists originally thought. Paleontologists now think that salamanders were living there before the islands separated from the rest of the Americas. Fossils like this help scientists understand where amphibians once lived and what Earth looked like long ago.

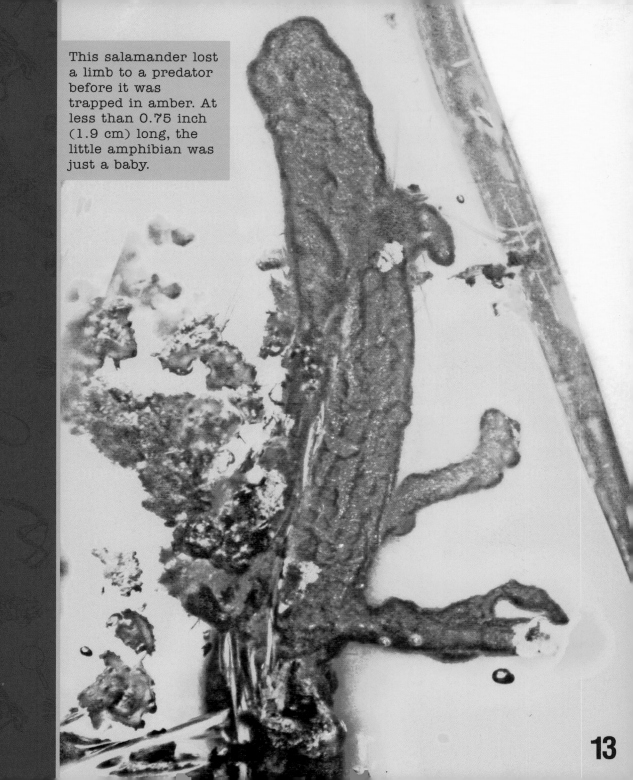

This salamander lost a limb to a predator before it was trapped in amber. At less than 0.75 inch (1.9 cm) long, the little amphibian was just a baby.

ROCK LAYERS

When paleontologists dig for fossils, they're also exploring the different rock layers where the fossils are found. Each rock layer formed over millions of years when existing earth was covered with a new layer of sediment or lava. The bodies of many organisms were covered up in the process. Over time, the sediment turned to rock and some animal remains became fossils.

Each rock layer represents a distinct period in history. One layer may have formed at the bottom of the ocean when sediment settled. The next layer might have formed millions of years later when a volcano erupted and lava flowed into the ocean, covering the previous layer.

Dig It!

Nearly 40 layers of sedimentary rock form the walls of the Grand Canyon. The oldest fossils found there are up to 1.2 billion years old!

fossilized footprints of a possible amphibian found at the Grand Canyon

It's easy to see where the different layers start and stop in the walls of the Grand Canyon. One layer is believed to have been part of an ancient riverbed. It contains amphibian fossils that are about 285 million years old.

HOW OLD IS IT?

Paleontologists use two methods to date, or figure out the age of, a fossil. The first is called relative dating. This method uses clues from the fossil's surroundings. If a fossil is found in a rock layer located deep within Earth, it must be older than fossils found in the upper layers. This is because the bottom layers had to be there before other layers could be deposited over them.

To estimate the age of a fossil based on rock layers, paleontologists use what are called "index fossils." These are common fossils that are easily recognizable and have already been dated. If a fossil is found in the same layer as an index fossil, chances are the two organisms lived around the same time.

Mucrospirifer mucronatus is an index fossil from the Devonian period (between about 419 million and 358 million years ago). Around this time, about 368 million years ago, prehistoric amphibians first began to appear.

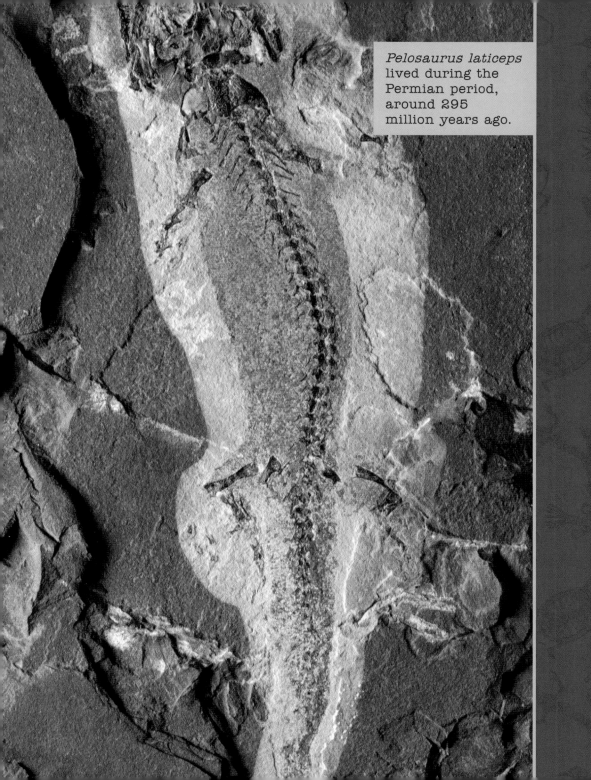

Pelosaurus laticeps lived during the Permian period, around 295 million years ago.

The second method scientists use to determine the age of fossils is called absolute dating. Unlike relative dating, which uses the **chronological** order of fossils, absolute dating is a more exact method of finding a fossil's age.

One important technique used in absolute dating is **radioactive** dating. Radioactive dating is the process in which scientists use half-lives to measure the radioactive elements, such as carbon-14, in a fossil. A half-life is the length of time it takes for half of that carbon to turn into **nitrogen**. Scientists know how long this takes—5,730 years! So, if the amounts of carbon and nitrogen in a fossil are equal, we know that one half-life has gone by and the fossil is about 5,730 years old.

When Matters More Than Where

The **geological time scale** (GTS) shows how rock layers that share the same index fossils are from the same time period, regardless of where they're found on Earth. This helps scientists determine when certain time periods began and ended. The GTS also shows how fossilized plants or animals follow each other through time in an orderly way. For example, a modern-day salamander fossil wouldn't be found in the same rock layer as its ancient ancestor *Elginerpeton pancheni*.

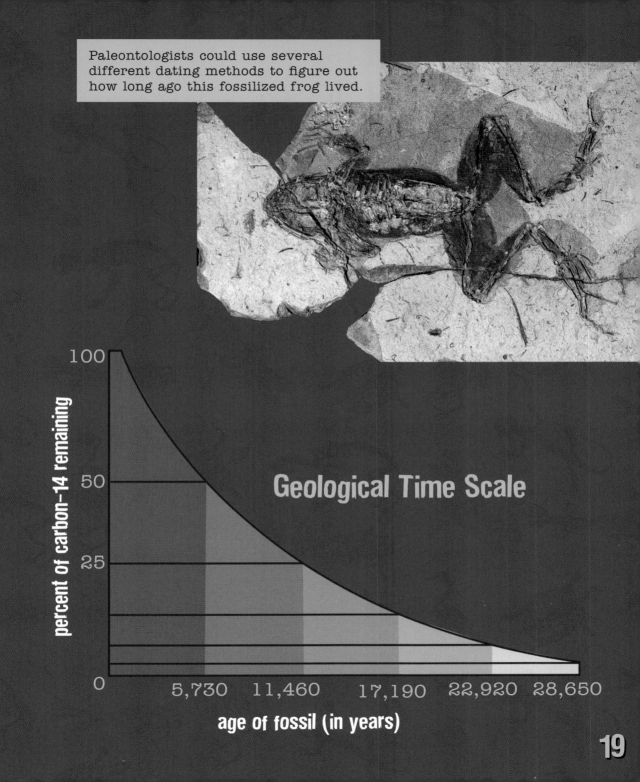

Paleontologists could use several different dating methods to figure out how long ago this fossilized frog lived.

Geological Time Scale

percent of carbon-14 remaining

100

50

25

0

5,730   11,460   17,190   22,920   28,650

age of fossil (in years)

EARLY FROGS AND SALAMANDERS

The *Gerobatrachus hottoni* fossil was found in Texas in the 1990s. Its frog-like head and salamander-like body puzzled scientists. Little was known about this organism until 2004 when scientists decided to study the fossil further. Since then, they have spent years trying to understand this strange organism.

Some scientists say *Gerobatrachus hottoni* could be an ancient amphibian that has no living relatives. Others believe it's a missing link in amphibian evolution. This idea suggests that frogs and salamanders branched off from their ancient amphibian ancestor at some point, while the wormlike **caecilians** descended from a different amphibian. *Gerobatrachus hottoni* may be the last common ancestor of frogs and salamanders. This would make it a close relative of lissamphibians, the subclass to which scientists believe all modern amphibians belong.

The "frogamander" is still full of mystery as scientists work to figure out how and where it fits in the amphibian family tree.

rendering of *Gerobatrachus hottoni*

Dig It!

Paleontologists fondly refer to the *Gerobatrachus hottoni* as a "frogamander" because of its frog-like head and salamander-like body.

TIGER SALAMANDERS AND MORE

In 2010, a bulldozer operator working in Snowmass Village, Colorado, made an amazing fossil discovery. Scientists arrived and dug up thousands of fossils from 50 species dating back 140,000 to 77,000 years. This was one of the most diverse, or varied, collections of Ice Age fossils ever found.

Mammoth and mastodon bones were both found at the Snowmass Village dig site. These mammals lived around the same time but didn't live in the same types of areas. This meant the landscape had changed from a forest (where mastodons lived) to a meadow (where mammoths lived). Scientists also recovered more than 22,000 tiger salamander bones spanning the entire date range, which indicates that these amphibians lived in both types of areas. The tiger salamander fossils were of the same species we see today.

tiger salamander

Paleontologists at the Snowmass Village dig site found a tiger salamander skeleton inside a mastodon tusk. The little amphibian must have taken shelter there before it was buried.

PIECING TOGETHER THE PUZZLE

What do paleontologists do with 22,000 ancient salamander fossils? They try to put them together! At least 500 individual salamanders were discovered at the Snowmass Village site. Putting these fossil puzzles together takes time, effort, and modern **technology**. Computers have helped paleontologists create models and fill in missing pieces to form complete skeletons.

Computed tomography (CT) scans create detailed images of fossils without damaging the original samples. This is especially important for amphibian fossils because many are tiny and delicate. They are often only a small piece of the animal. A CT scan allows scientists to build a complete digital model while keeping the original fossil safe. As technology advances, scientists learn more about fossils without having to use damaging methods like in the past.

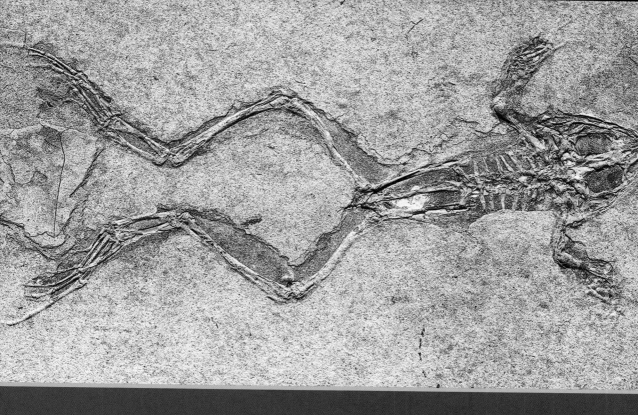

Scientists use computers to create digital models, like this frog skeleton, based off fossil records and CT scans.

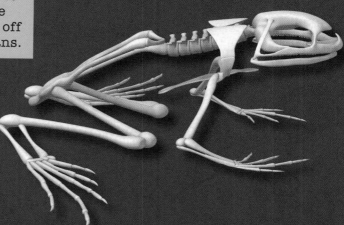

THAT'S NOT AN ALLIGATOR!

Not all amphibians were as small as the frogs and salamanders you see today. For example, *Eryops megacephalus* measured 5 to 6 feet (1.5 to 1.8 m) in length. This big amphibian lived between 299 and 251 million years ago. Fossils have been found in Texas and New Mexico.

Eryops megacephalus looked a lot like a modern-day alligator and weighed about 200 pounds (90.7 kg). Fossilized bones show that it had a strong, sturdy skeleton to carry around its heavy body. Because of its shape and large size, *Eryops megacephalus* likely didn't spend much time out of the water. However, scientists believe it to be among the first amphibians to thrive on land.

Dig It!

Eryops megacephalus lived long before dinosaurs evolved and was one of the largest land animals of its time.

Even its skeleton looks strong
and sturdy. *Eryops megacephalus*
definitely resembles the modern-day
alligator, but it wasn't a reptile.

CAECILIANS

A lesser-known group of amphibians are the caecilians. These legless, slimy creatures live mostly hidden from our view. Most use their strong skulls to burrow underground. Some live in water instead. Smaller caecilian species closely resemble earthworms, while larger caecilians are often mistaken for snakes.

Ancient caecilians are not easy for paleontologists to study because their fossils are difficult to find. This is likely because their skeletons are small and delicate. However, the discovery of 40 skulls and skeleton pieces in the early 1990s in northeastern Arizona made a huge difference in what we know about these creatures. These fossils were of *Eocaecilia micropodia*, which is the oldest known caecilian. These creatures lived 190 million years ago. After studying these fossils, scientists now believe that some early caecilians once had tiny limbs.

Definitely Not Snakes

Even though they look alike, amphibious caecilians and reptilian snakes have some striking differences. Caecilians have lots of tiny, sharp teeth, and snakes have fewer. Though they both have eyes, caecilians' eyes are covered by bone or skin and are mostly useless, whereas snakes can see. Many snakes have venom but most caecilians are toxic to eat, making them a poor choice for a predator's meal.

rendering of *Eocaecilia micropodia*

Caecilians can't hear, but scientists think they can sense vibrations using special organs in their ears.

CONNECTING PAST AND PRESENT

Triadobatrachus massinoti is an early frog-like creature. Its only fossil dates back 250 million years and was found in the 1930s on the island of Madagascar off the coast of Africa. It's considered a **transitional** fossil. Transitional fossils provide scientists with information about how one species evolved into another. *Triadobatrachus massinoti* was starting to show signs of change, such as a shorter tail. It helped fill in some of the blanks in amphibian evolution and serves as a link between primitive and modern-day frogs.

Uncovering more amphibian fossils will reveal additional information about how these creatures evolved. Advances in biology, **engineering**, and technology help scientists learn more than ever. Important details we couldn't see before are getting clearer and clearer, and the amphibian family tree is taking shape.

GLOSSARY

caecilians: Smooth, limbless amphibians that burrow underground or live underwater.

chronological: Based on time order.

computed tomography (CT) scan: A series of X-ray images taken from different angles that are combined to create a detailed cross-section image of an organism's body.

engineering: The study and practice of using math and science to do useful things.

evolve: To grow and change over time.

geological time scale (GTS): A system of measurement that relates rock layers to time and is used by scientists to describe events in Earth's history.

nitrogen: A gas with no taste or smell that makes up a large part of Earth's atmosphere and is present in all living things.

radioactive: Giving off rays of light, heat, or energy.

sediment: Matter such as rocks, sand, and small stones that is moved and deposited by water, wind, or glaciers.

technology: A method that uses science to solve problems and the tools used to solve those problems.

transitional: Passing from one state, stage, or place to another.

vertebrate: An animal that has a backbone.

INDEX

WEBSITES

Due to the changing nature of Internet links, PowerKids
Press has developed an online list of websites related to the
subject of this book. This site is updated regularly. Please use this
link to access the list: www.powerkidslinks.com/ff/amph